Muscle Building Cookbook

Fuel Your Workouts with Nutritious and Delicious Recipes

Logan Judge

Table of the Contents

Introduction

Welcome to our muscle-building cookbook! Whether you're a seasoned athlete or just starting out on your fitness journey, proper nutrition is key to reaching your goals. That's why we've put together a collection of delicious and nutritious recipes designed to help you build muscle and reach your peak performance. From high-protein breakfasts to post-workout snacks and hearty entrees, you'll find everything you need to fuel your body and reach your full potential. So, let's get cooking and take your muscle gains to the next level!

A muscle-building diet is a nutritional plan that focuses on providing the right amount and type of nutrients to support muscle growth and repair. This type of diet typically includes a balance of high-quality proteins, complex carbohydrates, and healthy fats.

Here are some tips for creating a muscle-building diet:

1. Consume Enough Protein: Protein is essential for building and repairing muscle tissue, so it's important to include plenty of high-quality protein sources in your diet. Good protein sources include lean meats, poultry, fish, eggs, dairy products, and plant-based protein sources such as beans, lentils, and tofu.

2. Increase Carbohydrate Intake: Carbohydrates are an important source of energy for your body and are crucial for muscle building. Choose complex carbohydrates such as whole grains, fruits, and vegetables to provide a steady supply of energy throughout the day.

3. Include Healthy Fats: Healthy fats such as olive oil, avocados, nuts, and seeds are important for overall health and also help with muscle building. Fat also provides a longer-lasting energy source and helps keep you feeling full and satisfied between meals.

4. Stay Hydrated: Drinking plenty of water is crucial for muscle building and overall health. Aim to drink at least eight glasses of water per day.

5. Eat Regularly: Eating small, frequent meals throughout the day can help keep your energy levels stable and

provide a constant supply of nutrients to support muscle growth.

6. Limit Processed Foods and Sugars: Processed foods and added sugars can add empty calories to your diet and can interfere with muscle building by providing a quick burst of energy followed by a sugar crash.

By following these guidelines and eating a balanced, nutritious diet, you can provide your body with the nutrients it needs to build muscle and achieve your fitness goals.

Breakfast

Protein-Packed Oatmeal Breakfast Bowl

Ingredients:

- 1 cup rolled oats
- 1 cup almond milk
- 1 scoop vanilla protein powder
- 1/2 banana, sliced
- 1/4 cup almonds, chopped
- 1 tbsp honey

Instructions:

1. In a medium saucepan, combine the oats and almond milk and cook over medium heat, stirring frequently, until the oats are soft and the mixture is thick, about 5 minutes.
2. Stir in the protein powder until well combined.
3. Transfer the oatmeal mixture to a bowl and top with the sliced banana, chopped almonds, and honey.
4. Serve and enjoy your delicious and nutritious breakfast!

Nutrition Information (per serving):

- ✓ Calories: 550
- ✓ Protein: 30g
- ✓ Carbohydrates: 66g
- ✓ Fat: 20g
- ✓ Fiber: 9g"

Peanut Butter and Banana Smoothie Bowl

Ingredients:

- 1 banana, frozen
- 1 scoop peanut butter flavored protein powder
- 1 cup almond milk
- 1 tsp honey
- 1 tbsp peanut butter
- 1/4 cup granola

Instructions:

1. In a blender, combine the frozen banana, protein powder, almond milk, and honey. Blend until smooth.

2. Pour the smoothie into a bowl and top with the peanut butter and granola.

3. Serve and enjoy your delicious and nutritious breakfast!

Nutrition Information (per serving):

- ✓ Calories: 460
- ✓ Protein: 30g
- ✓ Carbohydrates: 46g
- ✓ Fat: 20g
- ✓ Fiber: 6g

Egg and Veggie Breakfast Burrito

Ingredients:

- 2 eggs
- 1/2 cup chopped bell peppers
- 1/2 cup chopped onions

- 1/4 cup diced tomatoes

- 1/4 cup shredded cheese

- 1 whole grain tortilla

- Salt and pepper, to taste

Instructions:

1. In a non-stick pan, cook the eggs over medium heat until fully cooked. Season with salt and pepper.

2. In a separate pan, sauté the bell peppers and onions until softened, about 5 minutes.

3. Lay the tortilla flat and spread the cheese on top.

4. Add the cooked eggs, sautéed veggies, and diced tomatoes to the center of the tortilla.

5. Roll up the tortilla and serve warm.

Nutrition Information (per serving):

- ✓ Calories: 300

- ✓ Protein: 20g

- ✓ Carbohydrates: 30g

- ✓ Fat: 13g

- ✓ Fiber: 4g"

Power Protein Pancakes

Ingredients:

- 1 cup all-purpose flour
- 1 scoop vanilla protein powder
- 2 tbsp sugar
- 2 tsp baking powder
- 1/4 tsp salt
- 1 cup almond milk
- 1 egg
- 1 tsp vanilla extract
- 2 tbsp unsalted butter

Instructions:

1. In a large bowl, whisk together the flour, protein powder, sugar, baking powder, and salt.
2. In a separate bowl, beat together the almond milk, egg, and vanilla extract.
3. Add the wet ingredients to the dry ingredients and stir until just combined.
4. Heat a non-stick pan over medium heat and melt the butter.

5. Pour 1/4 cup of batter onto the pan for each pancake and cook until bubbles form on the surface and the edges start to dry, about 2-3 minutes.

6. Flip and cook for an additional 1-2 minutes on the other side.

7. Serve with your favorite toppings and enjoy your delicious and nutritious breakfast!

Nutrition Information (per serving, 2 pancakes):

- ✓ Calories: 400
- ✓ Protein: 20g
- ✓ Carbohydrates: 47g
- ✓ Fat: 17g
- ✓ Fiber: 2g

Savory Greek Yogurt and Veggie Breakfast Bowl

Ingredients:

- 1 cup Greek yogurt
- 1/2 cup chopped cherry tomatoes
- 1/2 cup chopped cucumber

- 1/4 cup crumbled feta cheese

- 1/4 cup chopped Kalamata olives

- Salt and pepper, to taste

Instructions:

1. In a large bowl, combine the Greek yogurt, cherry tomatoes, cucumber, feta cheese, and Kalamata olives.
2. Season with salt and pepper, to taste.
3. Serve and enjoy your delicious and nutritious breakfast!

Nutrition Information (per serving):

- ✓ Calories: 250
- ✓ Protein: 20g
- ✓ Carbohydrates: 12g
- ✓ Fat: 15g
- ✓ Fiber: 2g"

Oatmeal and Berry Power Bowl

Ingredients:

- 1 cup rolled oats
- 1 scoop vanilla protein powder
- 2 cups almond milk
- 1 cup mixed berries (strawberries, blueberries, raspberries)
- 2 tbsp honey
- 1 tsp vanilla extract
- 1 tbsp chopped almonds

Instructions:

1. In a saucepan, bring the oats, protein powder, and almond milk to a boil.
2. Reduce the heat to low and cook for 3-5 minutes, stirring occasionally, until the oats are fully cooked.
3. Stir in the mixed berries, honey, and vanilla extract.
4. Pour the oatmeal into a bowl and top with the chopped almonds.
5. Serve and enjoy your delicious and nutritious breakfast!

Nutrition Information (per serving):

- ✓ Calories: 500
- ✓ Protein: 30g
- ✓ Carbohydrates: 70g
- ✓ Fat: 16g
- ✓ Fiber: 10g

Egg and Avocado Toast

Ingredients:

- 2 whole grain slices of bread
- 1 ripe avocado
- 2 eggs
- Salt and pepper, to taste

Instructions:

1. Toast the bread to your desired level of crispiness.
2. Mash the avocado and spread it evenly on top of the toast.

3. In a non-stick pan, cook the eggs over medium heat until fully cooked. Season with salt and pepper.

4. Place the cooked eggs on top of the avocado toast.

5. Serve and enjoy your delicious and nutritious breakfast!

Nutrition Information (per serving):

- ✓ Calories: 400
- ✓ Protein: 20g
- ✓ Carbohydrates: 40g
- ✓ Fat: 20g
- ✓ Fiber: 10g"

Peanut Butter Banana Protein Smoothie I

Ingredients:

- 1 ripe banana
- 1 scoop vanilla protein powder
- 2 tbsp peanut butter
- 1 cup almond milk
- 1 tsp honey

- 1 tsp vanilla extract
- 1 cup ice

Instructions:

1. Blend all ingredients together in a blender until smooth.
2. Pour the smoothie into a glass and enjoy!

Nutrition Information (per serving):

- ✓ Calories: 450
- ✓ Protein: 30g
- ✓ Carbohydrates: 48g
- ✓ Fat: 20g
- ✓ Fiber: 4g

Egg White and Veggie Breakfast Wrap

Ingredients:

- 4 egg whites
- 1/4 cup diced bell peppers

- 1/4 cup diced onions
- 1/4 cup diced mushrooms
- Salt and pepper, to taste
- 2 whole grain tortillas
- 1/4 cup shredded cheese

Instructions:

1. In a non-stick pan, cook the egg whites with the bell peppers, onions, and mushrooms until fully cooked. Season with salt and pepper.
2. Lay out the tortillas and divide the egg and veggie mixture evenly between them.
3. Sprinkle the shredded cheese on top.
4. Roll up the tortillas and serve.

Nutrition Information (per serving):

- ✓ Calories: 400
- ✓ Protein: 20g
- ✓ Carbohydrates: 40g
- ✓ Fat: 15g
- ✓ Fiber: 6g"

Greek Yogurt and Berry Parfait

Ingredients:

- 1 cup plain Greek yogurt
- 1 cup mixed berries (strawberries, blueberries, raspberries)
- 1/4 cup granola
- 1 tbsp honey

Instructions:

1. In a tall glass or parfait dish, layer the Greek yogurt, mixed berries, and granola.
2. Drizzle honey over the top.
3. Repeat the layering until all ingredients are used up.
4. Serve and enjoy your delicious and nutritious breakfast!

Nutrition Information (per serving):

- ✓ Calories: 400
- ✓ Protein: 20g
- ✓ Carbohydrates: 48g
- ✓ Fat: 16g
- ✓ Fiber: 6g

Protein Pancakes

Ingredients:

- 1 scoop vanilla protein powder
- 1/2 cup whole wheat flour
- 1 tsp baking powder
- 1/4 tsp salt
- 1 egg
- 1/2 cup almond milk
- 1 tbsp melted coconut oil
- 1 tsp vanilla extract

Instructions:

1. In a mixing bowl, whisk together the protein powder, flour, baking powder, and salt.
2. In a separate bowl, whisk together the egg, almond milk, melted coconut oil, and vanilla extract.
3. Pour the wet ingredients into the dry ingredients and mix until just combined.
4. Heat a non-stick pan over medium heat and scoop 1/4 cup batter per pancake.

5. Cook the pancakes until bubbles form on the surface, then flip and cook for another minute or so.

6. Serve and enjoy your delicious and nutritious breakfast!

Nutrition Information (per serving, 2 pancakes):

- ✓ Calories: 400
- ✓ Protein: 20g
- ✓ Carbohydrates: 40g
- ✓ Fat: 20g
- ✓ Fiber: 4g"

Egg and Veggie Breakfast Bowl

Ingredients:

- 2 large eggs
- 1 cup chopped vegetables (bell peppers, onions, mushrooms)
- 1 tbsp olive oil
- Salt and pepper, to taste

- 1 whole grain English muffin, toasted
- 1 avocado, sliced

Instructions:

1. In a non-stick pan, heat the olive oil over medium heat.
2. Add the chopped vegetables to the pan and cook until they are tender, about 5 minutes.
3. Crack the eggs into the pan and cook until the whites are set and the yolks are still runny.
4. Season the eggs and vegetables with salt and pepper to taste.
5. Toast the English muffin and top it with the avocado slices.
6. Serve the eggs and veggies on top of the English muffin and avocado.
7. Enjoy your nutritious and delicious breakfast bowl!

Nutrition Information (per serving):

- ✓ Calories: 400
- ✓ Protein: 18g
- ✓ Carbohydrates: 36g
- ✓ Fat: 25g

✓ Fiber: 9g

Oatmeal Protein Power Bowl

Ingredients:

- 1 cup rolled oats
- 1 scoop vanilla protein powder
- 1 cup almond milk
- 1 banana, sliced
- 1 tbsp chopped walnuts
- 1 tsp honey

Instructions:

1. In a medium saucepan, bring the almond milk to a boil.
2. Stir in the oats and protein powder, and reduce heat to medium-low.
3. Cook the oatmeal, stirring occasionally, until it is thick and creamy, about 5 minutes.

4. Remove the oatmeal from heat and stir in the sliced banana.

5. Top the oatmeal with the chopped walnuts and drizzle with honey.

6. Serve and enjoy your delicious and nutritious breakfast bowl!

Nutrition Information (per serving):

- ✓ Calories: 400
- ✓ Protein: 20g
- ✓ Carbohydrates: 56g
- ✓ Fat: 14g
- ✓ Fiber: 6g"

Peanut Butter Banana Protein Smoothie II

Ingredients:

- 1 ripe banana
- 1 scoop vanilla protein powder

- 1 cup unsweetened almond milk

- 2 tbsp peanut butter

- 1 tsp honey

- 4 ice cubes

Instructions:

1. Place all ingredients in a blender and blend until smooth.

2. Pour the smoothie into a glass and enjoy your delicious and nutritious breakfast!

Nutrition Information (per serving):

- ✓ Calories: 380

- ✓ Protein: 28g

- ✓ Carbohydrates: 39g

- ✓ Fat: 18g

- ✓ Fiber: 4g

Ingredients:

- 1 cup plain Greek yogurt
- 1 scoop vanilla protein powder
- 1 cup mixed berries
- 1 tbsp chia seeds
- 1 tbsp honey

Instructions:

1. In a medium bowl, stir together the Greek yogurt and protein powder until well combined.
2. Layer the yogurt mixture, mixed berries, and chia seeds in a clear glass.
3. Repeat the layers until all ingredients are used.
4. Drizzle the honey over the top of the parfait.
5. Serve and enjoy your protein-packed breakfast!

Nutrition Information (per serving):

- ✓ Calories: 350
- ✓ Protein: 32g
- ✓ Carbohydrates: 43g

✓ Fat: 8g

✓ Fiber: 10g"

Blueberry Protein Pancakes

Ingredients:

- 1 cup whole wheat flour
- 2 scoops vanilla protein powder
- 2 tsp baking powder
- 1 egg
- 1 cup unsweetened almond milk
- 1 tbsp honey
- 1 tsp vanilla extract
- 1 cup fresh blueberries
- Cooking spray

Instructions:

1. In a large mixing bowl, combine the flour, protein powder, and baking powder.

2. In a separate bowl, beat the egg and then add the almond milk, honey, and vanilla extract.

3. Pour the wet ingredients into the dry ingredients and mix until just combined.

4. Gently fold in the blueberries.

5. Heat a non-stick pan over medium heat and spray with cooking spray.

6. Pour 1/4 cup of the batter onto the pan and cook until the edges start to dry and the top is bubbly.

7. Flip and cook until the other side is golden brown.

8. Repeat with the remaining batter.

9. Serve and enjoy your delicious protein-packed breakfast!

Nutrition Information (per serving, 2 pancakes):

- ✓ Calories: 420
- ✓ Protein: 30g
- ✓ Carbohydrates: 57g
- ✓ Fat: 9g
- ✓ Fiber: 6g

Egg and Turkey Sausage Breakfast Bowl

Ingredients:

- 4 turkey sausage links
- 4 large eggs
- 1 tbsp olive oil
- Salt and pepper to taste
- 1 avocado, diced
- 1/4 cup shredded cheddar cheese

Instructions:

1. Heat a large skillet over medium heat and add the turkey sausage links.
2. Cook until browned on both sides, about 5-7 minutes.
3. Remove from the skillet and set aside.
4. In the same skillet, add the olive oil and crack the eggs into the pan.
5. Cook until the whites are set and the yolks are still runny, about 3-4 minutes.
6. Season with salt and pepper to taste.
7. Serve the eggs and turkey sausage in bowls and top with diced avocado and shredded cheddar cheese.

8. Enjoy your protein-packed and delicious breakfast!

Nutrition Information (per serving):

- ✓ Calories: 550
- ✓ Protein: 30g
- ✓ Carbohydrates: 8g
- ✓ Fat: 45g
- ✓ Fiber: 5g"

Peanut Butter and Banana Oatmeal

Ingredients:

- 1 cup of rolled oats
- 1 ripe banana
- 2 tablespoons of creamy peanut butter
- 1 cup of almond milk
- 1 teaspoon of honey
- 1 teaspoon of cinnamon

Instructions:

1. Add the oats to a medium-sized saucepan.

2. Pour in the almond milk and add the cinnamon.

3. Place the saucepan on medium heat and cook the oats, stirring occasionally, until they are tender and most of the liquid is absorbed.

4. In a separate small bowl, mash the ripe banana with a fork.

5. Stir the mashed banana into the cooked oats.

6. Stir in the peanut butter and honey.

7. Serve the oatmeal in a bowl and top with additional sliced bananas and a drizzle of honey, if desired.

- ✓ Calories: 420 (per serving)
- ✓ Protein: 15g
- ✓ Carbs: 61g
- ✓ Fat: 15g
- ✓ Fiber: 6g

Protein-Packed Yogurt Parfait

Ingredients:

- 1 cup of Greek yogurt
- 1/2 cup of mixed berries (strawberries, blueberries, and raspberries)
- 1/4 cup of almonds, chopped
- 2 tablespoons of honey
- 1 scoop of vanilla protein powder

Instructions:

1. In a bowl, mix together the Greek yogurt, honey, and vanilla protein powder.
2. In a tall glass or jar, layer the mixed berries and chopped almonds on the bottom.
3. Pour the yogurt mixture over the berries and almonds.
4. Repeat the layering until all ingredients are used.
5. Serve immediately and enjoy your protein-packed parfait.

- ✓ Calories: 400 calories (per serving)
- ✓ Protein: 25g
- ✓ Carbs: 47g

✓ Fat: 15g

✓ Fiber: 5g

Peanut Butter and Banana Smoothie

Ingredients:

- 1 banana
- 2 tablespoons of peanut butter
- 1 scoop of whey protein powder
- 1 cup of almond milk
- 1 handful of ice

Instructions:

1. Blend the banana, peanut butter, whey protein powder, and almond milk together in a blender until smooth.
2. Add the ice and blend again until smooth and creamy.
3. Pour the smoothie into a glass and enjoy!

✓ Calories: 450 calories

✓ Protein 36g

- ✓ Carbohydrates 40g
- ✓ Healthy Fats 20g

Egg and Avocado Toast

Ingredients:

- 2 slices of whole grain toast
- 1 avocado
- 2 eggs
- Salt and pepper to taste

Instructions:

1. Toast the slices of whole grain bread.
2. While the toast is toasting, slice the avocado in half and remove the pit.
3. In a small pan, scramble the eggs over medium heat until cooked through.
4. Spread the avocado on the toast and sprinkle with salt and pepper.

5. Top each slice of toast with the scrambled eggs and
   serve.

✓ Calories: 500
✓ Protein 20g
✓ Carbohydrates 40g
✓ Healthy Fats 35g

Smoothie

Protein-Packed Berry Smoothie

Ingredients:

- 1 scoop of vanilla protein powder
- 1 cup mixed berries (strawberries, blueberries, raspberries)
- 1 banana
- 1 cup almond milk
- 1 teaspoon honey
- 1 cup ice

Instructions:

1. Add all ingredients to a blender and blend until smooth.
2. Pour the mixture into a glass and enjoy immediately.

Nutrition Information (per serving):

- ✓ Calories: 220
- ✓ Total Fat: 5g
- ✓ Total Carbohydrates: 30g

✓ Dietary Fiber: 4g

✓ Protein: 20g

Green Power Smoothie

Ingredients:

- 1 scoop of vanilla protein powder
- 1 banana
- 1 cup spinach
- 1 cup kale
- 1 cup almond milk
- 1 teaspoon honey
- 1 cup ice

Instructions:

1. Add all ingredients to a blender and blend until smooth.
2. Pour the mixture into a glass and enjoy immediately.

Nutrition Information (per serving):

✓ Calories: 200

✓ Total Fat: 5g

✓ Total Carbohydrates: 30g

✓ Dietary Fiber: 4g

✓ Protein: 20g

Chocolate Peanut Butter Protein Smoothie I

Ingredients:

- 1 scoop chocolate protein powder
- 1 ripe banana
- 1 tablespoon peanut butter
- 1 cup almond milk
- 1/2 cup ice

Instructions:

1. Add all ingredients to a blender.
2. Blend until smooth.
3. Pour into a glass and enjoy immediately.

Nutritional Information:

- ✓ Calories: 375
- ✓ Total Fat: 16g
- ✓ Saturated Fat: 3g
- ✓ Cholesterol: 3mg
- ✓ Sodium: 380mg
- ✓ Total Carbohydrates: 33g
- ✓ Dietary Fiber: 6g
- ✓ Total Sugars: 15g
- ✓ Protein: 28g

Berry Banana Protein Smoothie

Ingredients:

- 1 scoop vanilla protein powder
- 1 cup mixed berries (strawberries, blueberries, and raspberries)
- 1 ripe banana
- 1 cup almond milk

- 1/2 cup ice

Instructions:

1. Add all ingredients to a blender.
2. Blend until smooth.
3. Pour into a glass and enjoy immediately.

Nutritional Information:

- ✓ Calories: 335
- ✓ Total Fat: 10g
- ✓ Saturated Fat: 1g
- ✓ Cholesterol: 3mg
- ✓ Sodium: 270mg
- ✓ Total Carbohydrates: 45g
- ✓ Dietary Fiber: 8g
- ✓ Total Sugars: 26g
- ✓ Protein: 28g

Mango Pineapple Protein Smoothie

Ingredients:

- 1 scoop vanilla protein powder
- 1 cup frozen mango chunks
- 1 cup frozen pineapple chunks
- 1 cup coconut milk
- 1/2 cup ice

Instructions:

1. Add all ingredients to a blender.
2. Blend until smooth.
3. Pour into a glass and enjoy immediately.

Nutritional Information:

- ✓ Calories: 345
- ✓ Total Fat: 24g
- ✓ Saturated Fat: 21g
- ✓ Cholesterol: 0mg
- ✓ Sodium: 140mg
- ✓ Total Carbohydrates: 27g
- ✓ Dietary Fiber: 3g

✓ Total Sugars: 21g

✓ Protein: 13g

Spinach Avocado Protein Smoothie

Ingredients:

- 1 scoop vanilla protein powder
- 1 cup fresh spinach leaves
- 1 ripe avocado
- 1 cup almond milk
- 1/2 cup ice

Instructions:

1. Add all ingredients to a blender.
2. Blend until smooth.
3. Pour into a glass and enjoy immediately.

Nutritional Information:

✓ Calories: 420

✓ Total Fat: 33g

✓ Saturated Fat: 4g

✓ Cholesterol: 0mg

✓ Sodium: 350mg

✓ Total Carbohydrates: 19g

✓ Dietary Fiber: 13g

✓ Total Sugars: 3g

✓ Protein: 17g

Banana Oatmeal Protein Smoothie

Ingredients:

- 1 scoop vanilla protein powder
- 1 ripe banana
- 1/2 cup rolled oats
- 1 cup almond milk
- 1/2 cup ice

Instructions:

1. Add all ingredients to a blender.

2. Blend until smooth.

3. Pour into a glass and enjoy immediately.

Nutritional Information:

- ✓ Calories: 400
- ✓ Total Fat: 12g
- ✓ Saturated Fat: 1g
- ✓ Cholesterol: 0mg
- ✓ Sodium: 360mg
- ✓ Total Carbohydrates: 56g
- ✓ Dietary Fiber: 8g
- ✓ Total Sugars: 19g
- ✓ Protein: 27g

Strawberry Almond Protein Smoothie

Ingredients:

- 1 scoop strawberry protein powder

- 1 cup frozen strawberries

- 1 tablespoon almond butter

- 1 cup almond milk

- 1/2 cup ice

Instructions:

1. Add all ingredients to a blender.

2. Blend until smooth.

3. Pour into a glass and enjoy immediately.

Nutritional Information:

- ✓ Calories: 380

- ✓ Total Fat: 26g

- ✓ Saturated Fat: 2g

- ✓ Cholesterol: 0mg

- ✓ Sodium: 270mg

- ✓ Total Carbohydrates: 25g

- ✓ Dietary Fiber: 6g

- ✓ Total Sugars: 14g

- ✓ Protein: 17g

Green Protein Smoothie

Ingredients:

- 1 scoop vanilla protein powder
- 1 cup fresh spinach leaves
- 1 ripe banana
- 1/2 avocado
- 1 cup almond milk
- 1/2 cup ice

Instructions:

1. Add all ingredients to a blender.
2. Blend until smooth.
3. Pour into a glass and enjoy immediately.

Nutritional Information:

- ✓ Calories: 470
- ✓ Total Fat: 31g
- ✓ Saturated Fat: 4g
- ✓ Cholesterol: 0mg
- ✓ Sodium: 380mg
- ✓ Total Carbohydrates: 34g

- ✓ Dietary Fiber: 12g
- ✓ Total Sugars: 10g
- ✓ Protein: 27g

Sweet Potato Protein Smoothie

Ingredients:

- 1 scoop vanilla protein powder
- 1 cup cooked and cooled sweet potato
- 1 ripe banana
- 1 cup almond milk
- 1/2 cup ice

Instructions:

1. Add all ingredients to a blender.
2. Blend until smooth.
3. Pour into a glass and enjoy immediately.

Nutritional Information:

- ✓ Calories: 400

- ✓ Total Fat: 12g

- ✓ Saturated Fat: 1g

- ✓ Cholesterol: 0mg

- ✓ Sodium: 380mg

- ✓ Total Carbohydrates: 66g

- ✓ Dietary Fiber: 8g

- ✓ Total Sugars: 25g

- ✓ Protein: 27g

Chocolate Peanut Butter Protein Smoothie

Ingredients:

- 1 scoop chocolate protein powder

- 2 tablespoons peanut butter

- 1 ripe banana

- 1 cup almond milk

- 1/2 cup ice

Instructions:

1. Add all ingredients to a blender.
2. Blend until smooth.
3. Pour into a glass and enjoy immediately.

Nutritional Information:

- ✓ Calories: 500
- ✓ Total Fat: 34g
- ✓ Saturated Fat: 6g
- ✓ Cholesterol: 0mg
- ✓ Sodium: 380mg
- ✓ Total Carbohydrates: 35g
- ✓ Dietary Fiber: 6g
- ✓ Total Sugars: 18g
- ✓ Protein: 27g

Blueberry Vanilla Protein Smoothie

Ingredients:

- 1 scoop vanilla protein powder
- 1 cup fresh blueberries
- 1 ripe banana
- 1 cup almond milk
- 1/2 cup ice

Instructions:

1. Add all ingredients to a blender.
2. Blend until smooth.
3. Pour into a glass and enjoy immediately.

Nutritional Information:

- ✓ Calories: 420
- ✓ Total Fat: 12g
- ✓ Saturated Fat: 1g
- ✓ Cholesterol: 0mg
- ✓ Sodium: 380mg
- ✓ Total Carbohydrates: 66g
- ✓ Dietary Fiber: 8g

✓ Total Sugars: 34g

✓ Protein: 27g

Strawberry Protein Smoothie

Ingredients:

- 1 cup of fresh strawberries
- 1 scoop of vanilla protein powder
- 1/2 cup of plain Greek yogurt
- 1/4 cup of unsweetened almond milk
- 1 tsp of honey (optional)
- 2-3 ice cubes

Instructions:

1. Blend the strawberries, protein powder, Greek yogurt, almond milk, honey (if using), and ice cubes in a blender until smooth.
2. Pour the mixture into a glass and serve immediately.

- ✓ Calories: 200
- ✓ Total Fat: 6g
- ✓ Protein: 20g
- ✓ Carbohydrates: 21g

Strawberry Greek Yogurt Protein Smoothie

Ingredients:

- 1 cup of fresh strawberries
- 1 scoop of vanilla protein powder
- 1 cup of Greek yogurt
- 1/2 cup of unsweetened almond milk
- 1/2 teaspoon of honey (optional)
- 1 cup of ice

Instructions:

Start by adding the strawberries, protein powder, Greek yogurt, almond milk, and honey (if using) to a blender.

Add the ice and blend until smooth.

Pour into a glass and enjoy your delicious and nutritious smoothie.

- ✓ Calories: 300-350 calories per serving
- ✓ Protein 30g
- ✓ Carbohydrates 25g
- ✓ Fat 10g

Ingredients:

- 1 ripe banana
- 1 scoop of vanilla protein powder
- 1 tablespoon of peanut butter
- 1 cup of unsweetened almond milk
- 1/2 teaspoon of honey (optional)
- A handful of ice cubes

Instructions:

1. Add the banana, protein powder, peanut butter, almond milk, honey (if using), and ice cubes to a blender.
2. Blend on high speed until smooth and creamy.
3. Pour the smoothie into a glass and enjoy immediately.

- ✓ Calories: 400
- ✓ Protein: 28g
- ✓ Carbs: 42g
- ✓ Fat: 18g

Mixed Berry Protein Smoothie

Ingredients:

- 1 cup mixed berries (fresh or frozen)
- 1 scoop vanilla protein powder
- 1 cup unsweetened almond milk
- 1 teaspoon honey (optional)
- 3 ice cubes

Instructions:

1. In a blender, combine the mixed berries, protein powder, almond milk, and honey (if using).
2. Blend on high speed until smooth.
3. Add the ice cubes and blend until the ice is crushed.
4. Pour the smoothie into a glass and serve immediately.

✓ Calories: approximately 200
✓ Protein: 26 g
✓ Carbohydrates: 28 g
✓ Fat: 5 g

Ingredients:

- 1 cup fresh spinach
- 1 ripe avocado
- 1 scoop vanilla protein powder
- 1 cup unsweetened almond milk
- 1 teaspoon honey (optional)
- 3 ice cubes

Instructions:

1. In a blender, combine the spinach, avocado, protein powder, almond milk, and honey (if using).
2. Blend on high speed until smooth.
3. Add the ice cubes and blend until the ice is crushed.
4. Pour the smoothie into a glass and serve immediately.

Calories: approximately 300 Nutritional Values:

- ✓ Protein: 26 g
- ✓ Carbohydrates: 20 g
- ✓ Fat: 20 g

Chocolate and Banana Protein Smoothie

Ingredients:

- 1 medium ripe banana
- 1 scoop chocolate protein powder
- 1 cup unsweetened almond milk
- 1 tablespoon cocoa powder
- 1 teaspoon honey (optional)
- 3 ice cubes

Instructions:

1. In a blender, combine the banana, protein powder, almond milk, cocoa powder, and honey (if using).
2. Blend on high speed until smooth.
3. Add the ice cubes and blend until the ice is crushed.
4. Pour the smoothie into a glass and serve immediately.

Calories: approximately 250 Nutritional Values:

- ✓ Protein: 26 g
- ✓ Carbohydrates: 27 g
- ✓ Fat: 11 g

Chocolate Almond Protein Smoothie

Ingredients:

- 1 cup unsweetened almond milk
- 1 scoop chocolate protein powder
- 1 banana
- 2 tablespoons almonds
- 1 tablespoon unsweetened cocoa powder
- 1 teaspoon honey (optional)
- 4-5 ice cubes

Instructions:

1. Add the almond milk, protein powder, banana, almonds, cocoa powder, and honey to a blender.
2. Blend on high speed for about 30 seconds or until smooth.
3. Add ice cubes to the blender and blend for another 10-15 seconds.
4. Pour the smoothie into a glass and enjoy!

✓ Calories: 300
✓ Total Fat: 15g

✓ Total Carbohydrates: 30g

✓ Protein: 20g

Blueberry Coconut Protein Smoothie

Ingredients:

- 1 cup frozen blueberries
- 1 scoop vanilla protein powder
- 1/2 cup unsweetened coconut milk
- 1/2 cup Greek yogurt
- 1 tablespoon coconut flakes
- 1 teaspoon honey (optional)
- 4-5 ice cubes

Instructions:

1. Add the blueberries, protein powder, coconut milk, Greek yogurt, coconut flakes, and honey to a blender.
2. Blend on high speed for about 30 seconds or until smooth.

3. Add ice cubes to the blender and blend for another 10-15 seconds.

4. Pour the smoothie into a glass and enjoy!

✓ Calories: 300

✓ Total Fat: 20g

✓ Total Carbohydrates: 20g

✓ Protein: 20g

Pineapple Ginger Protein Smoothie

Ingredients:

- 1 cup pineapple chunks, frozen
- 1 scoop vanilla protein powder
- 1/2 cup unsweetened almond milk
- 1/2 cup Greek yogurt
- 1 teaspoon freshly grated ginger
- 1 teaspoon honey (optional)
- 4-5 ice cubes

Instructions:

1. Add the pineapple, protein powder, almond milk, Greek yogurt, ginger, and honey to a blender.
2. Blend on high speed for about 30 seconds or until smooth.
3. Add ice cubes to the blender and blend for another 10-15 seconds.
4. Pour the smoothie into a glass and enjoy!

- ✓ Calories: 300
- ✓ Total Fat: 10g
- ✓ Total Carbohydrates: 30g
- ✓ Protein: 20g

Chocolate-Covered Strawberry Protein Smoothie

Ingredients:

- 1 cup frozen strawberries
- 1 banana

- 1 scoop chocolate protein powder

- 1 cup unsweetened almond milk

- 1 tablespoon chia seeds

- 1 teaspoon honey (optional)

Instructions:

1. Add the frozen strawberries, banana, chocolate protein powder, unsweetened almond milk, chia seeds, and honey (if using) to a blender.
2. Blend on high speed until smooth and creamy.
3. Pour the smoothie into a glass and enjoy!

✓ Calories: Approximately 250

✓ Protein: 20g

✓ Carbohydrates: 40g

✓ Fat: 7g

✓ Fiber: 7g

Mango-Pineapple Protein Smoothie

Ingredients:

- 1 cup frozen mango
- 1 cup frozen pineapple
- 1 scoop vanilla protein powder
- 1 cup unsweetened coconut milk
- 1 tablespoon flaxseed meal
- 1 teaspoon agave nectar (optional)

Instructions:

1. Add the frozen mango, frozen pineapple, vanilla protein powder, unsweetened coconut milk, flaxseed meal, and agave nectar (if using) to a blender.
2. Blend on high speed until smooth and creamy.
3. Pour the smoothie into a glass and enjoy!

- ✓ Calories: Approximately 250
- ✓ Protein: 20g
- ✓ Carbohydrates: 40g
- ✓ Fat: 7g
- ✓ Fiber: 7g

Lunch

Grilled Chicken and Vegetable Skewers

Ingredients:

- 1 pound boneless, skinless chicken breasts, cut into 1-inch pieces
- 1 red bell pepper, cut into 1-inch pieces
- 1 yellow onion, cut into 1-inch pieces
- 1 zucchini, cut into 1-inch pieces
- 1 yellow squash, cut into 1-inch pieces
- 2 tablespoons olive oil
- Salt and pepper, to taste
- 8 metal or wooden skewers (soaked in water for 30 minutes if using wooden skewers)

Instructions:

1. Preheat a grill to medium-high heat.
2. In a large bowl, toss together the chicken, red bell pepper, yellow onion, zucchini, yellow squash, olive oil, salt, and pepper.

3. Divide the mixture evenly among the 8 skewers.

4. Place the skewers on the grill and cook, turning occasionally, until the chicken is cooked through and the vegetables are charred and tender, about 10-12 minutes.

5. Serve the skewers hot with a side of quinoa or brown rice.

Calories: Approximately 350 Nutritional Values (per serving):

✓ Protein: 35g

✓ Carbohydrates: 15g

✓ Fat: 17g

✓ Fiber: 4g

Tuna and Avocado Salad

Ingredients:

- 2 cans of tuna, drained

- 2 ripe avocados, diced

- 1/2 red onion, finely chopped

- 1/2 cup cherry tomatoes, halved
- 1/4 cup fresh cilantro, chopped
- 2 tablespoons lemon juice
- 2 tablespoons olive oil
- Salt and pepper, to taste

Instructions:

1. In a large bowl, combine the tuna, avocado, red onion, cherry tomatoes, and cilantro.
2. In a small bowl, whisk together the lemon juice, olive oil, salt, and pepper.
3. Pour the dressing over the tuna and avocado mixture and toss to combine.
4. Serve the salad over a bed of mixed greens or in a sandwich.

Calories: Approximately 400 Nutritional Values (per serving):

- ✓ Protein: 25g
- ✓ Carbohydrates: 20g
- ✓ Fat: 28g
- ✓ Fiber: 9

Turkey and Quinoa Stuffed Bell Peppers

Ingredients:

- 4 large bell peppers (any color), halved and seeded
- 1 pound ground turkey
- 1 cup cooked quinoa
- 1 can of diced tomatoes
- 1/2 red onion, diced
- 1 cup of corn kernels
- 1/4 cup of fresh cilantro, chopped
- 1 teaspoon cumin
- 1 teaspoon chili powder
- Salt and pepper, to taste

Instructions:

1. Preheat the oven to 375°F (190°C).
2. In a large skillet, cook the ground turkey over medium heat until browned, breaking it up into small pieces as it cooks.
3. Stir in the quinoa, diced tomatoes, red onion, corn, cilantro, cumin, chili powder, salt, and pepper. Cook for an additional 2-3 minutes.

4. Spoon the turkey and quinoa mixture evenly into the pepper halves.

5. Place the filled pepper halves in a 9x13 inch baking dish.

6. Bake the peppers for 20-25 minutes, or until the peppers are tender and the filling is hot.

7. Serve the stuffed peppers hot with a side of mixed greens or a fresh salad.

Calories: Approximately 400 Nutritional Values (per serving):

- ✓ Protein: 35g
- ✓ Carbohydrates: 40g
- ✓ Fat: 10g
- ✓ Fiber: 8g

Grilled Steak Salad with Feta and Walnuts

Ingredients:

- 1 pound flank steak
- Salt and pepper, to taste
- 2 heads of romaine lettuce, chopped
- 1/2 cup cherry tomatoes, halved

- 1/2 red onion, sliced
- 1/2 cup crumbled feta cheese
- 1/2 cup toasted walnuts
- 2 tablespoons balsamic vinaigrette

Instructions:

1. Preheat a grill to medium-high heat.
2. Season the flank steak with salt and pepper.
3. Place the steak on the grill and cook for 4-5 minutes per side, or until the desired degree of doneness is reached.
4. Remove the steak from the grill and let it rest for 5 minutes.
5. In a large bowl, toss together the romaine lettuce, cherry tomatoes, red onion, feta cheese, and walnuts.
6. Thinly slice the rested steak and add it to the salad.
7. Drizzle the balsamic vinaigrette over the salad and toss to combine.
8. Serve the salad immediately.

Calories: Approximately 550 Nutritional Values (per serving):

- ✓ Protein: 35g
- ✓ Carbohydrates: 15g

✓ Fat: 40g

✓ Fiber: 5g

Chicken and Vegetable Stir-Fry

Ingredients:

- 1 pound boneless, skinless chicken breast, sliced into thin strips
- 1 red bell pepper, sliced
- 1 yellow onion, sliced
- 1 cup broccoli florets
- 1 cup sliced mushrooms
- 2 cloves garlic, minced
- 1 teaspoon ginger, grated
- 2 tablespoons low-sodium soy sauce
- 2 tablespoons hoisin sauce
- 2 tablespoons olive oil
- Salt and pepper, to taste
- Cooked brown rice, for serving

Instructions:

1. In a small bowl, whisk together the soy sauce, hoisin sauce, and 1 tablespoon of the olive oil.
2. In a large skillet or wok, heat the remaining 1 tablespoon of olive oil over high heat.
3. Add the chicken strips to the skillet and cook until browned, about 3-4 minutes. Remove from the skillet and set aside.
4. In the same skillet, add the red bell pepper, yellow onion, broccoli, mushrooms, garlic, and ginger. Cook until the vegetables are just tender, about 5-7 minutes.
5. Return the cooked chicken to the skillet and stir in the soy sauce mixture.
6. Cook until the chicken is heated through and the sauce has thickened, about 2-3 minutes.
7. Season with salt and pepper, to taste.
8. Serve the stir-fry over cooked brown rice.

Calories: Approximately 500 Nutritional Values (per serving):

- ✓ Protein: 35g
- ✓ Carbohydrates: 50g
- ✓ Fat: 15g

✓ Fiber: 10g

Tuna Salad Wrap

Tuna Salad Wrap

Ingredients:

- 2 cans of water-packed tuna, drained
- 1/4 cup mayonnaise
- 1/4 cup chopped red onion
- 2 stalks celery, chopped
- 1/4 cup chopped dill pickles
- Salt and pepper, to taste
- 4 large whole grain wraps
- 4 leaves of lettuce
- 1 tomato, sliced

Instructions:

1. In a large bowl, mix together the tuna, mayonnaise, red onion, celery, dill pickles, salt, and pepper.
2. Lay out the wraps on a flat surface.

3. Place a lettuce leaf in the center of each wrap.

4. Spoon the tuna salad onto the lettuce leaves.

5. Top with the sliced tomato.

6. Roll up the wraps, tucking in the sides as you go.

7. Cut the wraps in half, if desired, and serve.

Calories: Approximately 400 Nutritional Values (per serving):

- ✓ Protein: 35g

- ✓ Carbohydrates: 40g

- ✓ Fat: 15g

- ✓ Fiber: 10g

Quinoa and Black Bean Bowl

Ingredients:

- 1 cup cooked quinoa

- 1 can of black beans, drained and rinsed

- 1 red bell pepper, diced

- 1 yellow corn, cooked and cut off the cob

- 1 avocado, diced
- 1/4 cup chopped cilantro
- 2 tablespoons lime juice
- 2 tablespoons olive oil
- Salt and pepper, to taste

Instructions:

1. In a large bowl, combine the cooked quinoa, black beans, red bell pepper, yellow corn, avocado, and cilantro.
2. In a small bowl, whisk together the lime juice, olive oil, salt, and pepper.
3. Pour the dressing over the quinoa mixture and stir to combine.
4. Serve the quinoa and black bean bowl at room temperature or chilled.

Calories: Approximately 500 Nutritional Values (per serving):

- ✓ Protein: 20g
- ✓ Carbohydrates: 50g
- ✓ Fat: 25g
- ✓ Fiber: 20g

Ingredients:

- 4 boneless, skinless chicken breasts
- Salt and pepper, to taste
- 2 heads of Romaine lettuce, chopped
- 1 cup cherry tomatoes, halved
- 1/2 cup crumbled feta cheese
- 1/4 cup chopped red onion
- 2 tablespoons balsamic vinegar
- 2 tablespoons olive oil

Instructions:

1. Preheat your grill to high heat.
2. Season the chicken breasts with salt and pepper.
3. Place the chicken on the grill and cook until browned and cooked through, about 6-8 minutes on each side.
4. In a large bowl, mix together the chopped Romaine lettuce, cherry tomatoes, feta cheese, and red onion.
5. In a small bowl, whisk together the balsamic vinegar and olive oil.

6. Cut the grilled chicken into slices and add to the salad mixture.

7. Pour the dressing over the salad and stir to combine.

8. Serve the grilled chicken salad immediately.

Calories: Approximately 400 Nutritional Values (per serving):

- ✓ Protein: 35g

- ✓ Carbohydrates: 15g

- ✓ Fat: 20g

- ✓ Fiber: 10g

Tuna Salad Lettuce Wraps

Ingredients:

- 2 cans of tuna, drained

- 1/4 cup mayonnaise

- 1/4 cup diced celery

- 1/4 cup diced red onion

- 1 tablespoon Dijon mustard

- Salt and pepper, to taste

- 8 leaves of butter lettuce
- 1 avocado, diced
- 1 lemon, juiced

Instructions:

1. In a medium bowl, combine the tuna, mayonnaise, celery, red onion, Dijon mustard, salt, and pepper. Stir to combine.
2. Rinse the butter lettuce leaves and pat dry.
3. Spoon a heaping tablespoon of the tuna salad into each lettuce leaf.
4. Top with diced avocado.
5. Squeeze lemon juice over the wraps.
6. Roll up the lettuce leaves and serve.

Calories: Approximately 300 Nutritional Values (per serving):

- ✓ Protein: 25g
- ✓ Carbohydrates: 10g
- ✓ Fat: 20g
- ✓ Fiber: 5g

Ingredients:

- 4 large red bell peppers
- 1 lb ground turkey
- 1 cup cooked brown rice
- 1 cup diced tomatoes
- 1/2 cup shredded cheddar cheese
- 1 tablespoon chili powder
- 1 teaspoon cumin
- Salt and pepper, to taste

Instructions:

1. Preheat the oven to 375°F (190°C).
2. Cut the tops off of the red bell peppers and remove the seeds and membranes.
3. In a large skillet, cook the ground turkey over medium heat until browned.
4. Add the cooked brown rice, diced tomatoes, shredded cheddar cheese, chili powder, cumin, salt, and pepper to the skillet. Stir to combine.
5. Fill each red bell pepper with the turkey and rice mixture.

6. Place the stuffed bell peppers in a baking dish and bake in the oven for 25-30 minutes, or until the peppers are tender and the cheese is melted.

7. Serve the stuffed bell peppers hot.

Calories: Approximately 400 Nutritional Values (per serving):

✓ Protein: 35g

✓ Carbohydrates: 40g

✓ Fat: 15g

✓ Fiber: 10g

Grilled Chicken and Quinoa Salad

Ingredients:

- 2 boneless, skinless chicken breasts
- Salt and pepper, to taste
- 1 cup cooked quinoa
- 1/2 cup diced red bell pepper
- 1/2 cup diced cucumber
- 1/4 cup diced red onion

- 1/4 cup crumbled feta cheese

- 2 tablespoons olive oil

- 1 tablespoon red wine vinegar

- 1 teaspoon Dijon mustard

- 1 teaspoon dried oregano

Instructions:

1. Season the chicken breasts with salt and pepper.

2. Heat a grill pan over medium heat and grill the chicken breasts for 6-8 minutes on each side, or until fully cooked.

3. In a large bowl, combine the cooked quinoa, red bell pepper, cucumber, red onion, feta cheese, olive oil, red wine vinegar, Dijon mustard, and dried oregano. Stir to combine.

4. Cut the grilled chicken into bite-sized pieces and add to the bowl with the quinoa mixture.

5. Serve the grilled chicken and quinoa salad at room temperature.

Calories: Approximately 400 Nutritional Values (per serving):

- ✓ Protein: 35g

✓ Carbohydrates: 40g

✓ Fat: 15g

✓ Fiber: 5g

Egg and Vegetable Protein Bowl

Ingredients:

- 4 large eggs
- 1 cup diced broccoli florets
- 1/2 cup diced red bell pepper
- 1/2 cup diced yellow squash
- 1 tablespoon olive oil
- Salt and pepper, to taste
- 1/4 cup crumbled feta cheese
- 2 tablespoons diced green onions

Instructions:

1. In a large skillet, heat the olive oil over medium heat.

2. Add the broccoli florets, red bell pepper, and yellow squash to the skillet. Season with salt and pepper.

3. Cook the vegetables for 5-7 minutes, or until tender.

4. In a separate pan, scramble the eggs over medium heat until fully cooked.

5. In a bowl, combine the cooked vegetables, scrambled eggs, crumbled feta cheese, and diced green onions. Stir to combine.

6. Serve the egg and vegetable protein bowl hot.

Calories: Approximately 300 Nutritional Values (per serving):

- ✓ Protein: 20g
- ✓ Carbohydrates: 20g
- ✓ Fat: 20g
- ✓ Fiber: 5g

Turkey and Avocado Lettuce Wraps

Ingredients:

- 4 ounces sliced turkey breast
- 2 ripe avocados, diced
- 4 large lettuce leaves
- 1/4 cup diced red onion
- 1/4 cup diced cherry tomatoes
- 2 tablespoons chopped fresh cilantro
- 1 tablespoon lime juice
- Salt and pepper, to taste

Instructions:

1. In a bowl, combine the diced avocados, red onion, cherry tomatoes, cilantro, lime juice, salt, and pepper. Stir to combine.
2. Lay out the lettuce leaves on a plate.
3. Top each lettuce leaf with a slice of turkey and a spoonful of the avocado mixture.
4. Roll up the lettuce leaves and secure with a toothpick, if desired.
5. Serve the turkey and avocado lettuce wraps immediately.

Calories: Approximately 250 Nutritional Values (per serving):

- ✓ Protein: 20g
- ✓ Carbohydrates: 15g
- ✓ Fat: 20g
- ✓ Fiber: 10g

Tuna Salad Stuffed Tomatoes

Ingredients:

- 2 cans of chunk light tuna in water, drained
- 2 ripe tomatoes
- 2 tablespoons mayonnaise
- 1 tablespoon dijon mustard
- 1/4 cup diced celery
- 1/4 cup diced red onion
- Salt and pepper, to taste

Instructions:

1. Cut the tops off the tomatoes and scoop out the seeds and flesh with a spoon. Reserve the scooped out tomato flesh for another use.

2. In a bowl, combine the tuna, mayonnaise, dijon mustard, celery, red onion, salt, and pepper. Stir to combine.

3. Spoon the tuna salad mixture into the hollowed-out tomatoes.

4. Serve the tuna salad stuffed tomatoes immediately.

Calories: Approximately 200 Nutritional Values (per serving):

✓ Protein: 20g

✓ Carbohydrates: 10g

✓ Fat: 10g

✓ Fiber: 5g

Grilled Chicken and Vegetable Skewers

Ingredients:

- 1 pound boneless, skinless chicken breast, cut into 1-inch cubes

- 1 red bell pepper, seeded and cut into 1-inch pieces
- 1 yellow bell pepper, seeded and cut into 1-inch pieces
- 1 zucchini, sliced
- 1 yellow squash, sliced
- 1/4 cup olive oil
- 2 cloves garlic, minced
- 1 teaspoon dried oregano
- 1 teaspoon dried thyme
- Salt and pepper, to taste
- Skewers (if using wooden skewers, soak in water for 30 minutes before using to prevent burning)

Instructions:

1. In a large bowl, combine the chicken, red bell pepper, yellow bell pepper, zucchini, yellow squash, olive oil, garlic, oregano, thyme, salt, and pepper. Stir to coat the chicken and vegetables evenly.
2. Thread the chicken and vegetables onto the skewers, alternating between chicken and vegetables.
3. Preheat a grill to medium-high heat. Grease the grates with cooking spray.

4. Grill the skewers for 10-12 minutes, or until the chicken is cooked through and the vegetables are tender, turning occasionally.

5. Serve the grilled chicken and vegetable skewers immediately.

Calories: Approximately 400 Nutritional Values (per serving):

- ✓ Protein: 30g
- ✓ Carbohydrates: 10g
- ✓ Fat: 30g
- ✓ Fiber: 5g

Quinoa and Black Bean Salad

Ingredients:

- 1 cup quinoa, rinsed and drained
- 1 can black beans, drained and rinsed
- 1 red bell pepper, diced
- 1 yellow bell pepper, diced

- 1/2 cup corn kernels (fresh or frozen)
- 1/4 cup chopped fresh cilantro
- 2 tablespoons lime juice
- 2 tablespoons olive oil
- Salt and pepper, to taste

Instructions:

1. In a saucepan, combine the quinoa with 2 cups of water. Bring to a boil, then reduce the heat to low, cover, and simmer for 18-20 minutes, or until the quinoa is tender and the water has been absorbed.
2. In a large bowl, combine the cooked quinoa, black beans, red bell pepper, yellow bell pepper, corn, cilantro, lime juice, olive oil, salt, and pepper. Stir to combine.
3. Serve the quinoa and black bean salad immediately, or store in an airtight container in the refrigerator for up to 4 days.

Calories: Approximately 400 Nutritional Values (per serving):

- ✓ Protein: 15g
- ✓ Carbohydrates: 50g
- ✓ Fat: 20g

Dinner

High-Protein Chicken Salad with Quinoa and Avocado

Ingredients:

- 2 chicken breasts, cooked and diced
- 1 cup cooked quinoa
- 1 avocado, diced
- 1/2 red bell pepper, diced
- 1/4 red onion, diced
- 1/4 cup diced cucumber
- 2 tablespoons olive oil
- 2 tablespoons lemon juice
- Salt and pepper, to taste
- 2 cups mixed greens

Instructions:

1. In a large bowl, combine cooked and diced chicken, cooked quinoa, diced avocado, red bell pepper, red onion, and cucumber.

2. In a separate small bowl, whisk together olive oil, lemon juice, salt, and pepper to make the dressing.

3. Pour the dressing over the chicken and quinoa mixture and toss to combine.

4. Serve the salad on a bed of mixed greens.

Nutrition Information:

- ✓ Servings: 2
- ✓ Calories: 725
- ✓ Total Fat: 43 g
- ✓ Saturated Fat: 8 g
- ✓ Cholesterol: 129 mg
- ✓ Sodium: 645 mg
- ✓ Total Carbohydrates: 44 g
- ✓ Dietary Fiber: 12 g
- ✓ Sugar: 5 g
- ✓ Protein: 47 g

Ingredients:

- 2 cans of tuna, drained
- 1 can of white beans, rinsed and drained
- 1/4 cup diced red onion
- 1/4 cup diced celery
- 2 tablespoons diced pickles
- 2 tablespoons mayonnaise
- 2 tablespoons Dijon mustard
- Salt and pepper, to taste
- 4 slices of sweet potato
- 1 tablespoon olive oil

Instructions:

1. In a large bowl, combine the drained tuna, white beans, red onion, celery, and pickles.
2. In a separate small bowl, whisk together mayonnaise, Dijon mustard, salt, and pepper to make the dressing.
3. Pour the dressing over the tuna and white bean mixture and toss to combine.

4. Preheat a pan over medium heat and brush both sides of the sweet potato slices with olive oil.

5. Cook the sweet potato slices for 3-4 minutes on each side, or until they are crispy and tender.

6. Serve the tuna and white bean salad on top of the sweet potato toast.

Nutrition Information:

- ✓ Servings: 2
- ✓ Calories: 624
- ✓ Total Fat: 33 g
- ✓ Saturated Fat: 5 g
- ✓ Cholesterol: 47 mg
- ✓ Sodium: 708 mg
- ✓ Total Carbohydrates: 43 g
- ✓ Dietary Fiber: 11 g
- ✓ Sugar: 7 g
- ✓ Protein: 42 g

Ingredients:

- 4 boneless, skinless chicken breasts
- 2 medium sweet potatoes, peeled and diced
- 3 cups broccoli florets
- 1 teaspoon olive oil
- Salt and pepper to taste
- 1 teaspoon paprika
- 1 teaspoon garlic powder

Instructions:

1. Preheat the oven to 400°F.
2. In a large mixing bowl, mix together the diced sweet potatoes, broccoli florets, olive oil, salt, pepper, paprika, and garlic powder.
3. Spread the mixture evenly in a single layer on a baking sheet.
4. Place the chicken breasts on top of the vegetables and sprinkle with a little more salt and pepper.
5. Bake for 25-30 minutes or until the chicken is cooked through and the vegetables are tender.

6. Serve the chicken and vegetables in bowls, with additional salt and pepper to taste.

✓ Calories: 450

✓ Fat: 11g

✓ Carbohydrates: 45g

✓ Protein: 40g

Grilled Salmon with Quinoa and Grilled Vegetables

Ingredients:

- 4 salmon fillets
- 2 cups cooked quinoa
- 2 bell peppers, sliced
- 1 onion, sliced
- 1 zucchini, sliced
- 1 yellow squash, sliced
- 1 tablespoon olive oil
- Salt and pepper to taste
- Lemon wedges, for serving

Instructions:

1. Heat a grill to high heat.
2. Brush the salmon fillets and vegetables with the olive oil and season with salt and pepper.
3. Grill the salmon fillets for 4-5 minutes on each side, or until fully cooked.
4. Grill the vegetables until they are slightly charred and tender, about 5-7 minutes.
5. Serve the salmon fillets with the cooked quinoa and grilled vegetables.
6. Squeeze lemon juice over the top of the dish, to taste.

- ✓ Calories: 500
- ✓ Fat: 25g
- ✓ Carbohydrates: 35g
- ✓ Protein: 40g

Ingredients:

- 4 boneless chicken breasts
- Salt and pepper, to taste
- Olive oil, for brushing
- 2 medium sweet potatoes, peeled and diced
- 1 red onion, diced
- 1 avocado, diced
- 2 tablespoons lemon juice
- 1/4 cup chopped fresh parsley
- 1/4 cup chopped fresh cilantro

Instructions:

1. Preheat grill to medium-high heat.
2. Season chicken breasts with salt and pepper. Lightly brush with olive oil.
3. Place chicken and sweet potatoes on the grill. Cook chicken for 6-8 minutes on each side or until fully cooked. Cook sweet potatoes until tender, about 8-10 minutes.

4. In a large bowl, combine cooked sweet potatoes, red onion, avocado, lemon juice, parsley, and cilantro. Season with salt and pepper to taste.

5. Serve chicken on top of sweet potato salad.

Calories: 466 Nutrition Information (per serving):

- ✓ Protein: 48g
- ✓ Carbs: 34g
- ✓ Fat: 19g

Turkey and Vegetable Stir-Fry

Ingredients:

- 1 pound ground turkey
- 1 red bell pepper, sliced
- 1 green bell pepper, sliced
- 1 yellow onion, sliced
- 2 cups broccoli florets
- 2 tablespoons olive oil

- Salt and pepper, to taste

- 2 tablespoons soy sauce

- 2 tablespoons hoisin sauce

Instructions:

1. In a large skillet, heat olive oil over medium heat.

2. Add ground turkey and cook until browned, breaking it apart with a spatula as it cooks.

3. Add sliced bell peppers, onion, and broccoli florets to the skillet. Cook until vegetables are tender, about 5-7 minutes.

4. Season with salt and pepper to taste. Stir in soy sauce and hoisin sauce.

5. Serve hot over a bed of rice or noodles.

Calories: 466 Nutrition Information (per serving):

- ✓ Protein: 48g

- ✓ Carbs: 34g

- ✓ Fat: 19g

Protein-Packed Chicken Salad Bowl

Ingredients:

- 2 boneless, skinless chicken breasts
- Salt and pepper, to taste
- 1 cup quinoa, cooked
- 1 cup mixed greens
- 1 cup cherry tomatoes, halved
- 1 avocado, sliced
- 1/4 cup red onion, sliced
- 1/4 cup walnuts, chopped
- 2 tablespoons olive oil
- 1 tablespoon lemon juice

Instructions:

1. Preheat oven to 400°F. Line a baking sheet with parchment paper.
2. Season chicken breasts with salt and pepper and place on the prepared baking sheet. Bake for 20-25 minutes, or until fully cooked.
3. Allow the chicken to cool and then slice it into thin pieces.

4. In a large bowl, combine the quinoa, mixed greens, cherry tomatoes, avocado, red onion, and walnuts.

5. Drizzle with olive oil and lemon juice and season with salt and pepper to taste.

6. Top with sliced chicken and serve.

Nutrition Information:

- ✓ Calories: 700
- ✓ Total Fat: 44g
- ✓ Saturated Fat: 8g
- ✓ Total Carbohydrates: 42g
- ✓ Protein: 37g
- ✓ Sodium: 260mg

Steak and Sweet Potato Bowl

Ingredients:

- 1 pound flank steak
- Salt and pepper, to taste
- 2 medium sweet potatoes, peeled and diced

- 1 tablespoon olive oil
- 1 cup cooked brown rice
- 1 cup steamed broccoli florets
- 1/4 cup red bell pepper, sliced
- 2 tablespoons balsamic vinegar
- 2 tablespoons soy sauce

Instructions:

1. Preheat oven to 400°F. Line a baking sheet with parchment paper.
2. Season the flank steak with salt and pepper and place on the prepared baking sheet. Bake for 15-20 minutes, or until fully cooked.
3. In a large bowl, toss the sweet potatoes with olive oil and season with salt and pepper. Spread on a separate baking sheet and bake for 25-30 minutes, or until tender and slightly crispy.
4. In a large bowl, combine the cooked brown rice, steamed broccoli, red bell pepper, balsamic vinegar, and soy sauce.
5. Slice the cooked steak and add it to the bowl.

6. Serve the steak and sweet potato mixture over the rice and broccoli mixture.

Nutrition Information:

- ✓ Calories: 600
- ✓ Total Fat: 29g
- ✓ Saturated Fat: 9g
- ✓ Total Carbohydrates: 49g
- ✓ Protein: 44g
- ✓ Sodium: 740mg

Grilled Chicken Breast with Sweet Potato and Broccoli

Ingredients:

- 4 boneless, skinless chicken breasts
- 1 teaspoon olive oil
- Salt and pepper to taste
- 2 medium sweet potatoes, peeled and cubed
- 2 cups broccoli florets

- 1 teaspoon paprika

- 1 teaspoon garlic powder

Instructions:

1. Preheat the grill to medium-high heat.

2. Season the chicken breasts with salt, pepper, paprika and garlic powder.

3. Brush the chicken with olive oil.

4. Place the chicken breasts on the grill and cook for 6-7 minutes on each side or until fully cooked.

5. While the chicken is cooking, steam the sweet potatoes and broccoli in a separate pot until tender.

6. Serve the chicken with the sweet potatoes and broccoli.

- ✓ Calories: approx. 450 calories per serving

- ✓ Nutritional information: high in protein, carbohydrates, fiber, vitamins A and C

Ingredients:

- 1 lb ground turkey
- 1 tablespoon olive oil
- 2 cups chopped vegetables of your choice (such as bell peppers, carrots, and onions)
- 1 garlic clove, minced
- 1 teaspoon ginger, grated
- 2 tablespoons low-sodium soy sauce
- 1 tablespoon cornstarch
- 1/4 cup water
- Rice or quinoa for serving

Instructions:

1. Heat a large wok or skillet over medium-high heat.
2. Add the ground turkey and cook until browned, breaking it up into small pieces as it cooks.
3. Remove the turkey from the pan and set it aside.
4. Add the olive oil to the pan, along with the vegetables. Cook until the vegetables are tender, about 5 minutes.

5. Add the garlic and ginger to the pan and cook for another minute.

6. Return the ground turkey to the pan and add the soy sauce.

7. In a small bowl, whisk together the cornstarch and water.

8. Add the cornstarch mixture to the pan and stir until the sauce thickens, about 2 minutes.

9. Serve the stir-fry over rice or quinoa.

✓ Calories: approx. 400 calories per serving

✓ Nutritional information: high in protein, fiber, and vitamins from the vegetables.

Baked Salmon with Quinoa and Asparagus

Ingredients:

- 4 salmon fillets
- 1 tablespoon olive oil
- Salt and pepper to taste
- 1 cup quinoa

- 2 cups water
- 1 bunch of asparagus
- 1 lemon, sliced

Instructions:

1. Preheat the oven to 400°F (200°C).
2. Line a baking sheet with parchment paper.
3. Place the salmon fillets on the prepared baking sheet.
4. Brush the salmon fillets with olive oil and sprinkle with salt and pepper.
5. Place the lemon slices on top of the salmon fillets.
6. Bake for 12-15 minutes or until the salmon is fully cooked.
7. While the salmon is cooking, rinse the quinoa and place it in a pot with 2 cups of water.
8. Bring the water to a boil, reduce heat and let it simmer for 15-20 minutes or until the quinoa is fully cooked.
9. Steam the asparagus until tender.
10. Serve the salmon with quinoa and asparagus on the side.

- ✓ Calories: approx. 550 calories per serving
- ✓ Nutritional information: high in protein, healthy fats, fiber, vitamins B and D

Ingredients:

- 1 lb ground turkey
- 1 egg
- 1/4 cup breadcrumbs
- 1 teaspoon garlic powder
- Salt and pepper to taste
- 2 medium sweet potatoes, peeled and sliced into fries
- 1 tablespoon olive oil
- Salad greens of your choice

Instructions:

1. Preheat the oven to 400°F (200°C).
2. In a large bowl, mix together the ground turkey, egg, breadcrumbs, garlic powder, salt, and pepper.
3. Form the mixture into 4 patties.
4. Place the sweet potato slices on a baking sheet and drizzle with olive oil.
5. Bake the sweet potato fries and turkey burgers for 25-30 minutes or until the turkey is fully cooked and the sweet potatoes are crispy.

6. Serve the turkey burgers with sweet potato fries and a side salad.

✓ Calories: approx. 550 calories per serving
✓ Nutritional information: high in protein, healthy carbohydrates, fiber, vitamins A and C

Beef and Vegetable Stir-Fry with Rice

Ingredients:

- 1 lb lean beef, sliced into thin strips
- 1 tablespoon olive oil
- 2 cups chopped vegetables of your choice (such as bell peppers, carrots, and onions)
- 1 garlic clove, minced
- 1 teaspoon ginger, grated
- 2 tablespoons low-sodium soy sauce
- 1 tablespoon cornstarch
- 1/4 cup water
- 2 cups cooked rice

Instructions:

1. Heat a large wok or skillet over medium-high heat.
2. Add the beef strips to the pan and cook until browned, about 5 minutes.
3. Remove the beef from the pan and set it aside.
4. Add the olive oil to the pan, along with the vegetables. Cook until the vegetables are tender, about 5 minutes.
5. Add the garlic and ginger to the pan and cook for another minute.
6. Return the beef to the pan and add the soy sauce.
7. In a small bowl, whisk together the cornstarch and water.
8. Add the cornstarch mixture to the pan and stir until the sauce thickens, about 2 minutes.
9. Serve the stir-fry over cooked rice.

✓ Calories: approx. 500 calories per serving
✓ Nutritional information: high in protein, fiber, and vitamins from the vegetables

Grilled Pork Chops with Mashed Sweet Potatoes and Steamed Broccoli

Ingredients:

- 4 boneless pork chops
- 1 teaspoon olive oil
- Salt and pepper to taste
- 2 medium sweet potatoes, peeled and cubed
- 2 cups broccoli florets
- 1 teaspoon paprika
- 1 teaspoon garlic powder

Instructions:

1. Preheat the grill to medium-high heat.
2. Season the pork chops with salt, pepper, paprika and garlic powder.
3. Brush the pork chops with olive oil.
4. Place the pork chops on the grill and cook for 6-7 minutes on each side or until fully cooked.
5. While the pork chops are cooking, boil the sweet potatoes until tender and then mash them.
6. Steam the broccoli until tender.

7. Serve the pork chops with the mashed sweet potatoes and steamed broccoli on the side.

✓ Calories: approx. 500 calories per serving
✓ Nutritional information: high in protein, healthy carbohydrates, fiber, vitamins A and C.

Chicken and Quinoa Salad with Avocado

Ingredients:

- 2 boneless chicken breasts
- 1 teaspoon olive oil
- Salt and pepper to taste
- 1 cup quinoa
- 2 cups chicken broth
- 1 large avocado, diced
- 1/4 cup red onion, diced
- 1 cup cherry tomatoes, halved
- 1/4 cup cilantro, chopped
- 1 lime, juiced

- 2 tablespoons honey
- 1 tablespoon dijon mustard
- 2 tablespoons apple cider vinegar

Instructions:

1. Preheat the oven to 400°F (200°C).
2. Season the chicken breasts with salt and pepper.
3. Heat a large oven-safe skillet over medium-high heat and add the olive oil.
4. Add the chicken breasts to the skillet and cook until browned, about 2-3 minutes on each side.
5. Transfer the skillet to the oven and bake for 15-20 minutes or until the chicken is fully cooked.
6. In a separate saucepan, cook the quinoa according to the instructions using chicken broth.
7. In a large bowl, combine the quinoa, avocado, red onion, cherry tomatoes, and cilantro.
8. In a small bowl, whisk together the lime juice, honey, dijon mustard, and apple cider vinegar.
9. Pour the dressing over the quinoa mixture and toss to combine.
10. Serve the salad with the chicken breasts on the side.

✓ Calories: approx. 550 calories per serving

✓ Nutritional information: high in protein, fiber, healthy fats, and vitamins from the vegetables

Grilled Salmon with Sweet Potato Fries and Grilled Asparagus

Ingredients:

- 4 salmon fillets
- 1 teaspoon olive oil
- Salt and pepper to taste
- 2 large sweet potatoes, sliced into fries
- 1 lb asparagus
- 1 teaspoon paprika
- 1 teaspoon garlic powder

Instructions:

1. Preheat the grill to medium-high heat.
2. Season the salmon fillets with salt, pepper, paprika and garlic powder.
3. Brush the salmon fillets with olive oil.

4. Place the salmon fillets and sweet potato fries on the grill and cook for 8-10 minutes on each side or until fully cooked.

5. While the salmon and sweet potatoes are cooking, grill the asparagus for 3-4 minutes or until tender.

6. Serve the salmon with the sweet potato fries and grilled asparagus on the side.

✓ Calories: approx. 550 calories per serving

✓ Nutritional information: high in protein, healthy fats, vitamins A and C, and fiber from the asparagus.

Beef and Vegetable Stir-Fry

Ingredients:

- 1 lb flank steak, sliced into thin strips
- 1 tablespoon olive oil
- Salt and pepper to taste
- 1 red bell pepper, sliced
- 1 yellow onion, sliced

- 1 zucchini, sliced
- 2 cloves garlic, minced
- 2 tablespoons soy sauce
- 2 tablespoons hoisin sauce
- 1 tablespoon honey
- 1 teaspoon cornstarch
- 2 cups cooked brown rice

Instructions:

1. Heat a large wok or skillet over high heat and add the olive oil.
2. Season the beef strips with salt and pepper and add them to the wok.
3. Cook the beef strips until browned, about 2-3 minutes.
4. Remove the beef strips from the wok and set aside.
5. Add the red bell pepper, yellow onion, zucchini, and garlic to the wok and stir-fry for 2-3 minutes.
6. Return the beef strips to the wok and add the soy sauce, hoisin sauce, honey, and cornstarch.
7. Stir everything together and continue cooking for another 2-3 minutes or until the sauce has thickened.
8. Serve the stir-fry over the cooked brown rice.

✓ Calories: approx. 600 calories per serving

✓ Nutritional information: high in protein, vitamins and minerals from the vegetables, and complex carbohydrates from the brown rice

Turkey and Rice Bowl with Roasted Vegetables

Ingredients:

- 1 lb ground turkey
- 1 tablespoon olive oil
- Salt and pepper to taste
- 1 teaspoon dried basil
- 1 teaspoon dried oregano
- 1 red bell pepper, sliced
- 1 yellow onion, sliced
- 2 cloves garlic, minced
- 2 cups cooked brown rice
- 2 cups mixed roasted vegetables (such as carrots, zucchini, and eggplant)

Instructions:

1. Preheat the oven to 400°F (200°C).
2. Heat a large skillet over medium-high heat and add the olive oil.
3. Add the ground turkey to the skillet and season with salt, pepper, basil, and oregano.
4. Cook the ground turkey until browned and fully cooked, about 10-15 minutes.
5. In a separate roasting pan, place the red bell pepper, yellow onion, and mixed vegetables.
6. Drizzle with olive oil and season with salt and pepper.
7. Roast in the oven for 20-25 minutes or until the vegetables are tender and slightly charred.
8. Serve the cooked turkey over the cooked brown rice, topped with the roasted vegetables.

✓ Calories: approx. 550 calories per serving
✓ Nutritional information: high in protein, vitamins and minerals from the vegetables, and complex carbohydrates from the brown rice

Ingredients:

- 4 boneless, skinless chicken breasts
- 1 tablespoon olive oil
- Salt and pepper to taste
- 2 medium sweet potatoes, peeled and diced
- 1 red onion, sliced
- 1 red bell pepper, sliced
- 2 cloves garlic, minced
- 2 tablespoons balsamic vinegar
- 2 tablespoons honey
- 2 tablespoons Dijon mustard
- 2 cups cooked quinoa

Instructions:

1. Preheat oven to 400°F (200°C).
2. In a large roasting pan, place the chicken breasts and drizzle with olive oil.
3. Season with salt and pepper and bake for 20-25 minutes or until fully cooked.

4. While the chicken is cooking, heat a large skillet over medium heat and add the diced sweet potatoes.

5. Cook the sweet potatoes for 5-7 minutes or until they start to soften.

6. Add the red onion, red bell pepper, and garlic to the skillet and continue cooking for another 2-3 minutes.

7. In a small bowl, whisk together the balsamic vinegar, honey, and Dijon mustard.

8. Pour the mixture over the vegetables and stir to combine.

9. Serve the roasted chicken over the cooked quinoa, topped with the sweet potato and vegetable mixture.

✓ Calories: approx. 600 calories per serving

✓ Nutritional information: high in protein from the chicken, complex carbohydrates from the quinoa, and vitamins and minerals from the sweet potatoes and vegetables.

Black Bean and Rice Bowl with Grilled Steak

Ingredients:

- 1 lb flank steak
- 1 tablespoon olive oil
- Salt and pepper to taste
- 1 red onion, sliced
- 1 red bell pepper, sliced
- 2 cloves garlic, minced
- 1 can black beans, drained and rinsed
- 2 cups cooked brown rice
- 2 tablespoons chili powder
- 2 tablespoons cumin
- 2 tablespoons paprika

Instructions:

1. Heat a large grill or grill pan over high heat.
2. Season the flank steak with salt and pepper and drizzle with olive oil.
3. Grill the steak for 4-5 minutes per side or until desired doneness is reached.
4. In a large skillet, heat the olive oil over medium heat.

5. Add the red onion, red bell pepper, and garlic to the skillet and cook for 2-3 minutes.

6. Add the black beans, cooked brown rice, chili powder, cumin, and paprika to the skillet.

7. Stir everything together and continue cooking for another 2-3 minutes.

8. Serve the grilled steak over the black bean and rice mixture.

✓ Calories: approx. 700 calories per serving

✓ Nutritional information: high in protein from the steak, complex carbohydrates from the brown rice, and fiber from the black beans.

Tuna and Vegetable Stir-Fry

Ingredients:

- 1 can of tuna, drained and flaked

- 2 tablespoons sesame oil

- 1 red bell pepper, sliced

- 1 yellow bell pepper, sliced
- 1 large carrot, sliced
- 1 large zucchini, sliced
- 1 red onion, sliced
- 2 cloves garlic, minced
- 2 tablespoons soy sauce
- 1 teaspoon honey
- 2 tablespoons hoisin sauce
- 2 cups cooked brown rice

Instructions:

1. In a large wok or skillet, heat the sesame oil over high heat.
2. Add the sliced red and yellow bell peppers, carrot, zucchini, and red onion to the wok.
3. Stir-fry the vegetables for 2-3 minutes or until they start to soften.
4. Add the minced garlic and stir-fry for another minute.
5. In a small bowl, whisk together the soy sauce, honey, and hoisin sauce.
6. Pour the sauce over the stir-fried vegetables and stir to combine.

7. Add the flaked tuna to the wok and stir everything together.

8. Serve the tuna and vegetable stir-fry over the cooked brown rice.

✓ Calories: approx. 550 calories per serving

✓ Nutritional information: high in protein from the tuna, complex carbohydrates from the brown rice, and vitamins and minerals from the vegetables.

Turkey and Avocado Sandwich with Sweet Potato Fries

Ingredients:

- 4 slices of whole grain bread
- 4 oz deli turkey meat
- 2 ripe avocados, mashed
- 2 tablespoons mayonnaise
- Salt and pepper to taste
- 2 medium sweet potatoes, peeled and sliced into thin rounds
- 1 tablespoon olive oil

Instructions:

1. In a small bowl, mix together the mashed avocados and mayonnaise.
2. Season with salt and pepper to taste.
3. Toast the slices of whole grain bread.
4. Spread the avocado mixture onto 2 slices of toast.
5. Place the deli turkey meat onto the avocado toast.
6. Top with the remaining 2 slices of toast to make 2 sandwiches.
7. Preheat oven to 400°F (200°C).
8. In a large bowl, mix the sliced sweet potatoes with olive oil.
9. Season with salt and pepper to taste.
10. Spread the sweet potato rounds in a single layer on a baking sheet.
11. Bake for 20-25 minutes or until crispy and golden brown.
12. Serve the turkey and avocado sandwich with the sweet potato fries on the side.

✓ Calories: approx. 700 calories per serving

✓ Nutritional information: high in protein from the turkey, healthy fats from the avocado, and complex carbohydrates and vitamins and minerals from the sweet potatoes.

Grilled Chicken and Vegetable Skewers

Ingredients:

- 4 boneless, skinless chicken breasts, cut into 1-inch cubes
- 2 red bell peppers, cut into 1-inch pieces
- 2 yellow onions, cut into 1-inch pieces
- 1 large zucchini, cut into 1-inch rounds
- 2 tablespoons olive oil
- 1 teaspoon dried basil
- 1 teaspoon dried oregano
- Salt and pepper to taste
- 4 skewers

Instructions:

1. Soak the skewers in water for 30 minutes to prevent burning.
2. In a large bowl, mix together the chicken cubes, red bell peppers, yellow onions, and zucchini.
3. Add the olive oil, dried basil, dried oregano, salt, and pepper to the bowl and mix to coat the chicken and vegetables evenly.
4. Thread the chicken and vegetable pieces onto the skewers, alternating the ingredients.
5. Preheat the grill to medium-high heat.
6. Grill the skewers for 10-12 minutes or until the chicken is cooked through and the vegetables are tender, turning occasionally.
7. Serve the grilled chicken and vegetable skewers with your favorite side dish.

✓ Calories: approx. 400 calories per serving
✓ Nutritional information: high in protein from the chicken, vitamins and minerals from the vegetables, and healthy fats from the olive oil.

Ingredients:

- 8 oz sirloin steak
- 2 tablespoons olive oil
- Salt and pepper to taste
- 4 cups mixed greens
- 1 red bell pepper, sliced
- 1 yellow onion, sliced
- 1 large zucchini, sliced
- 1 cup cherry tomatoes, halved
- 2 tablespoons balsamic vinegar
- 2 tablespoons Dijon mustard
- 2 tablespoons honey

Instructions:

1. Preheat the grill to high heat.
2. Brush the steak with olive oil and season with salt and pepper.
3. Grill the steak for 4-5 minutes on each side or until it reaches your desired level of doneness.
4. Preheat oven to 400°F (200°C).

5. In a large bowl, mix together the sliced red bell pepper, yellow onion, zucchini, and cherry tomatoes.

6. Add the remaining olive oil to the bowl and mix to coat the vegetables evenly.

7. Spread the vegetables in a single layer on a baking sheet.

8. Roast for 20-25 minutes or until the vegetables are tender and lightly browned.

9. In a small bowl, whisk together the balsamic vinegar, Dijon mustard, and honey.

10. In a large bowl, mix together the mixed greens, roasted vegetables, and balsamic dressing.

11. Serve the grilled steak on top of the mixed greens and vegetable salad.

✓ Calories: approx. 600 calories per serving

✓ Nutritional information: high in protein from the steak, vitamins and minerals from the mixed greens and roasted vegetables, and healthy fats from the olive oil.

Ingredients:

- 1 pound boneless, skinless chicken breast, cut into 1-inch cubes
- 1 cup uncooked white rice
- 2 tablespoons oil, divided
- 1 medium onion, sliced
- 2 garlic cloves, minced
- 2 medium carrots, sliced
- 1 red bell pepper, sliced
- 1 cup sliced mushrooms
- 2 tablespoons soy sauce
- 1 tablespoon cornstarch
- 1 tablespoon water
- Salt and pepper, to taste

Instructions:

1. Cook rice according to package instructions and set aside.

2. In a large pan, heat 1 tablespoon of oil over medium-high heat. Add chicken and cook for 5-7 minutes, or until browned. Remove from pan and set aside.

3. In the same pan, add the remaining oil and heat. Add onion, garlic, carrots, red bell pepper, and mushrooms. Stir-fry for 3-5 minutes or until vegetables are tender.

4. In a small bowl, mix soy sauce, cornstarch, and water.

5. Add the chicken back to the pan and add the soy sauce mixture. Stir-fry for another 2-3 minutes or until the sauce has thickened.

6. Serve the chicken stir-fry over the cooked rice.

Nutrition Information (per serving, based on 4 servings):

- ✓ Calories: 485
- ✓ Total Fat: 13 g
- ✓ Saturated Fat: 2 g
- ✓ Cholesterol: 96 mg
- ✓ Sodium: 739 mg
- ✓ Total Carbohydrates: 45 g
- ✓ Dietary Fiber: 4 g
- ✓ Sugars: 6 g
- ✓ Protein: 44 g

Beef and Sweet Potato Stir-Fry

Ingredients:

- 1 pound sirloin steak, sliced into thin strips
- 1 large sweet potato, peeled and sliced into 1/2-inch rounds
- 2 tablespoons oil, divided
- 1 medium onion, sliced
- 2 garlic cloves, minced
- 2 medium carrots, sliced
- 1 red bell pepper, sliced
- 2 tablespoons soy sauce
- 1 tablespoon cornstarch
- 1 tablespoon water
- Salt and pepper, to taste

Instructions:

1. In a large pan, heat 1 tablespoon of oil over medium-high heat. Add sweet potato and cook for 5-7 minutes, or until tender. Remove from pan and set aside.
2. In the same pan, add the remaining oil and heat. Add onion, garlic, carrots, red bell pepper, and steak strips.

Stir-fry for 3-5 minutes or until the steak is cooked through and vegetables are tender.

3. In a small bowl, mix soy sauce, cornstarch, and water.

4. Add the sweet potato back to the pan and add the soy sauce mixture. Stir-fry for another 2-3 minutes or until the sauce has thickened.

5. Serve the beef and sweet potato stir-fry over a bed of rice.

Nutrition Information (per serving, based on 4 servings):

- ✓ Calories: 547
- ✓ Total Fat: 20 g
- ✓ Saturated Fat: 5 g
- ✓ Cholesterol: 78 mg
- ✓ Sodium: 767 mg
- ✓ Total Carbohydrates: 42 g
- ✓ Dietary Fiber: 6 g
- ✓ Sugars: 9 g
- ✓ Protein: 49 g

Dessert

Peanut Butter Protein Cookies

Ingredients:

- 1 cup creamy peanut butter
- 1/2 cup brown sugar
- 1 large egg
- 1 tsp vanilla extract
- 1 scoop vanilla protein powder
- 1 tsp baking soda
- 1/4 tsp salt

Instructions:

1. Preheat the oven to 350°F (180°C). Line a baking sheet with parchment paper.
2. In a large mixing bowl, combine the peanut butter, brown sugar, egg, and vanilla extract. Beat until well combined.
3. Add the protein powder, baking soda, and salt to the bowl and mix until well combined.

4. Using a cookie scoop or spoon, drop dough onto the prepared baking sheet, spacing them 2 inches apart.

5. Bake for 12-15 minutes, or until the edges are lightly golden.

6. Remove from the oven and let cool on the baking sheet for 5 minutes before transferring to a wire rack to cool completely.

Nutrition information (per cookie):

- ✓ Calories: 150
- ✓ Protein: 8g
- ✓ Fat: 12g
- ✓ Carbohydrates: 9g

Chocolate Protein Brownies

Ingredients:

- 1 cup unsweetened cocoa powder
- 1/2 cup melted coconut oil

- 1 cup sugar
- 4 large eggs
- 2 tsp vanilla extract
- 1 scoop chocolate protein powder
- 1/2 tsp baking powder
- 1/4 tsp salt

Instructions:

1. Preheat the oven to 350°F (180°C). Line an 8x8 inch (20x20 cm) baking pan with parchment paper.
2. In a large mixing bowl, combine the cocoa powder, melted coconut oil, and sugar. Beat until well combined.
3. Add the eggs, vanilla extract, protein powder, baking powder, and salt to the bowl and mix until well combined.
4. Pour the batter into the prepared baking pan and smooth out the surface with a spatula.
5. Bake for 25-30 minutes, or until a toothpick inserted in the center comes out clean.
6. Remove from the oven and let cool completely in the pan before cutting into squares.

Nutrition information (per brownie):

- ✓ Calories: 200
- ✓ Protein: 8g
- ✓ Fat: 14g
- ✓ Carbohydrates: 15g

Protein-Packed Banana Oat Muffins

Ingredients:

- 1 1/2 cups rolled oats
- 1 ripe banana, mashed
- 1/2 cup vanilla protein powder
- 1 tsp baking powder
- 1/4 tsp salt
- 2 large eggs
- 1/2 cup almond milk
- 1 tsp vanilla extract
- 1/4 cup honey

Instructions:

1. Preheat the oven to 350°F (180°C). Line a muffin tin with muffin liners.

2. In a large mixing bowl, combine the oats, mashed banana, protein powder, baking powder, and salt. Stir until well combined.

3. In a separate bowl, beat the eggs and then add in the almond milk, vanilla extract, and honey. Whisk until well combined.

4. Add the wet ingredients to the dry ingredients and stir until just combined.

5. Divide the batter evenly between the muffin cups.

6. Bake for 18-20 minutes, or until a toothpick inserted into the center of a muffin comes out clean.

7. Remove from the oven and let cool in the muffin tin for 5 minutes before transferring to a wire rack to cool completely.

Nutrition information (per muffin):

✓ Calories: 150

✓ Protein: 10g

✓ Fat: 4g

✓ Carbohydrates: 22g

Protein-Packed Carrot Cake

Ingredients:

- 1 1/2 cups whole wheat flour
- 1 scoop vanilla protein powder
- 2 tsp baking powder
- 1 tsp cinnamon
- 1/2 tsp nutmeg
- 1/4 tsp salt
- 2 large eggs
- 1/2 cup almond milk
- 1 tsp vanilla extract
- 1/4 cup honey
- 1 cup grated carrots
- 1/2 cup chopped walnuts

Instructions:

1. Preheat the oven to 350°F (180°C). Line an 8x8 inch (20x20 cm) baking pan with parchment paper.
2. In a large mixing bowl, combine the flour, protein powder, baking powder, cinnamon, nutmeg, and salt. Stir until well combined.

3. In a separate bowl, beat the eggs and then add in the almond milk, vanilla extract, and honey. Whisk until well combined.

4. Add the wet ingredients to the dry ingredients and stir until just combined.

5. Fold in the grated carrots and chopped walnuts.

6. Pour the batter into the prepared baking pan and smooth out the surface with a spatula.

7. Bake for 25-30 minutes, or until a toothpick inserted into the center comes out clean.

8. Remove from the oven and let cool completely in the pan before cutting into squares.

Nutrition information (per square):

✓ Calories: 200

✓ Protein: 10g

✓ Fat: 9g

✓ Carbohydrates: 23g

Ingredients:

- 1 1/2 cups all-purpose flour
- 1 scoop vanilla protein powder
- 1 tsp baking powder
- 1/4 tsp salt
- 2 large eggs
- 1/2 cup almond milk
- 1/2 cup creamy peanut butter
- 1 tsp vanilla extract
- 1/4 cup honey
- 1/2 cup dark chocolate chips

Instructions:

1. Preheat the oven to 350°F (180°C). Line a muffin tin with muffin liners.
2. In a large mixing bowl, combine the flour, protein powder, baking powder, and salt. Stir until well combined.

3. In a separate bowl, beat the eggs and then add in the almond milk, peanut butter, vanilla extract, and honey. Whisk until well combined.

4. Add the wet ingredients to the dry ingredients and stir until just combined.

5. Fold in the chocolate chips.

6. Divide the batter evenly between the muffin cups.

7. Bake for 18-20 minutes, or until a toothpick inserted into the center of a muffin comes out clean.

8. Remove from the oven and let cool in the muffin tin for 5 minutes before transferring to a wire rack to cool completely.

Nutrition information (per cupcake):

- ✓ Calories: 300
- ✓ Protein: 15g
- ✓ Fat: 18g
- ✓ Carbohydrates: 25g

Protein-Packed Blueberry Cheesecake Bars

Ingredients:

- 1 1/2 cups graham cracker crumbs
- 1/4 cup melted butter
- 1 scoop vanilla protein powder
- 16 oz cream cheese, softened
- 1/4 cup honey
- 2 large eggs
- 1 tsp vanilla extract
- 1 cup fresh blueberries

Instructions:

1. Preheat the oven to 350°F (180°C). Line an 8x8 inch (20x20 cm) baking pan with parchment paper.
2. In a small mixing bowl, combine the graham cracker crumbs and melted butter. Stir until well combined.
3. Press the mixture into the bottom of the prepared baking pan to form a crust.
4. In a separate mixing bowl, beat the cream cheese and protein powder until well combined.

5. Add in the honey, eggs, and vanilla extract, and continue to beat until smooth.

6. Pour the mixture over the crust and smooth out the surface with a spatula.

7. Sprinkle the fresh blueberries over the top of the mixture.

8. Bake for 25-30 minutes, or until the edges are set and the center is slightly jiggly.

9. Remove from the oven and let cool completely in the pan before cutting into squares.

Nutrition information (per square):

- ✓ Calories: 270
- ✓ Protein: 15g
- ✓ Fat: 21g
- ✓ Carbohydrates: 16g

Protein-Packed Banana Bread Muffins

Ingredients:

- 1 1/2 cups all-purpose flour
- 1 scoop vanilla protein powder
- 1 tsp baking powder
- 1/4 tsp baking soda
- 1/4 tsp salt
- 2 ripe bananas, mashed
- 2 large eggs
- 1/4 cup unsweetened almond milk
- 1/4 cup melted coconut oil
- 1 tsp vanilla extract
- 1/4 cup honey

Instructions:

1. Preheat the oven to 350°F (180°C). Line a muffin tin with muffin liners.
2. In a large mixing bowl, combine the flour, protein powder, baking powder, baking soda, and salt. Stir until well combined.

3. In a separate bowl, combine the mashed bananas, eggs, almond milk, melted coconut oil, vanilla extract, and honey. Whisk until well combined.

4. Add the wet ingredients to the dry ingredients and stir until just combined.

5. Divide the batter evenly between the muffin cups.

6. Bake for 18-20 minutes, or until a toothpick inserted into the center of a muffin comes out clean.

7. Remove from the oven and let cool in the muffin tin for 5 minutes before transferring to a wire rack to cool completely.

Nutrition information (per muffin):

- ✓ Calories: 250
- ✓ Protein: 15g
- ✓ Fat: 13g
- ✓ Carbohydrates: 27g

Protein-Packed Carrot Cake Bars

Ingredients:

- 1 1/2 cups all-purpose flour
- 1 scoop vanilla protein powder
- 1 tsp baking powder
- 1 tsp cinnamon
- 1/4 tsp nutmeg
- 1/4 tsp salt
- 2 large eggs
- 1/4 cup unsweetened almond milk
- 1/4 cup melted coconut oil
- 1 tsp vanilla extract
- 1/4 cup honey
- 1 1/2 cups grated carrots
- 1/2 cup raisins
- 1/2 cup chopped walnuts

Instructions:

1. Preheat the oven to 350°F (180°C). Line an 8x8 inch (20x20 cm) baking pan with parchment paper.

2. In a large mixing bowl, combine the flour, protein powder, baking powder, cinnamon, nutmeg, and salt. Stir until well combined.

3. In a separate bowl, combine the eggs, almond milk, melted coconut oil, vanilla extract, and honey. Whisk until well combined.

4. Add the wet ingredients to the dry ingredients and stir until just combined.

5. Fold in the grated carrots, raisins, and chopped walnuts.

6. Pour the mixture into the prepared baking pan and smooth out the surface with a spatula.

7. Bake for 25-30 minutes, or until a toothpick inserted into the center of the bars comes out clean.

8. Remove from the oven and let cool completely in the pan before cutting into squares.

Nutrition information (per square):

- ✓ Calories: 270
- ✓ Protein: 15g
- ✓ Fat: 13g
- ✓ Carbohydrates: 30g

Chocolate Peanut Butter Protein Brownies

Ingredients:

- 1 cup whole wheat flour
- 1 scoop chocolate protein powder
- 1/2 cup unsweetened cocoa powder
- 1 tsp baking powder
- 1/4 tsp salt
- 1/2 cup creamy peanut butter
- 1/2 cup maple syrup
- 2 large eggs
- 1 tsp vanilla extract
- 1/2 cup unsweetened almond milk
- 1/2 cup dark chocolate chips

Instructions:

1. Preheat the oven to 350°F (180°C) and line an 8x8 inch (20x20 cm) baking pan with parchment paper.
2. In a large mixing bowl, combine the flour, protein powder, cocoa powder, baking powder, and salt. Stir until well combined.

3. In a separate bowl, whisk together the peanut butter,
   maple syrup, eggs, vanilla extract, and almond milk.

4. Add the wet ingredients to the dry ingredients and stir
   until just combined.

5. Fold in the dark chocolate chips.

6. Pour the mixture into the prepared baking pan and
   smooth out the surface with a spatula.

7. Bake for 20-25 minutes, or until a toothpick inserted into
   the center of the brownies comes out clean.

8. Remove from the oven and let cool completely in the
   pan before cutting into squares.

Nutrition information (per brownie):

✓ Calories: 320

✓ Protein: 15g

✓ Fat: 18g

✓ Carbohydrates: 29g

Ingredients:

- 1 1/2 cups all-purpose flour
- 1 scoop vanilla protein powder
- 1 tsp baking powder
- 1/4 tsp salt
- 1/2 cup unsalted butter, softened
- 1 cup granulated sugar
- 3 large eggs
- 2 tbsp freshly squeezed lemon juice
- 1 tsp lemon zest
- 1 tsp vanilla extract
- 1/2 cup unsweetened almond milk

Instructions:

1. Preheat the oven to 350°F (180°C) and grease a 9x5 inch (23x13 cm) loaf pan.
2. In a large mixing bowl, combine the flour, protein powder, baking powder, and salt. Stir until well combined.

3. In a separate bowl, cream together the butter and sugar until light and fluffy.

4. Beat in the eggs, one at a time, followed by the lemon juice, lemon zest, and vanilla extract.

5. Gradually add the dry ingredients to the wet ingredients, alternating with the almond milk, until just combined.

6. Pour the mixture into the prepared loaf pan and smooth out the surface with a spatula.

7. Bake for 50-60 minutes, or until a toothpick inserted into the center of the pound cake comes out clean.

8. Remove from the oven and let cool completely in the pan before slicing.

Nutrition information (per slice, based on 12 slices):

✓ Calories: 280

✓ Protein: 15g

✓ Fat: 12g

✓ Carbohydrates: 34g

Peanut Butter and Banana Protein Muffins

Ingredients:

- 2 ripe bananas, mashed
- 1/2 cup creamy peanut butter
- 2 eggs
- 1/2 cup almond milk
- 1 tsp vanilla extract
- 1/2 cup oat flour
- 1/2 cup whey protein powder
- 1 tsp baking powder
- 1/2 tsp baking soda
- 1/4 tsp salt
- 1/4 cup semi-sweet chocolate chips (optional)

Instructions:

1. Preheat the oven to 350°F and line a muffin tin with muffin cups.
2. In a large mixing bowl, mash the ripe bananas.
3. Add the peanut butter and mix until smooth.
4. Beat in the eggs, one at a time, until well combined.
5. Stir in the almond milk and vanilla extract.

6. In a separate bowl, whisk together the oat flour, whey protein powder, baking powder, baking soda, and salt.

7. Gradually add the dry ingredients to the banana mixture and stir until just combined.

8. Fold in the chocolate chips, if using.

9. Spoon the batter evenly into the muffin cups, filling each about 2/3 full.

10. Bake for 20-25 minutes, or until a toothpick inserted into the center of a muffin comes out clean.

11. Remove the muffins from the oven and let cool for 5 minutes in the tin, then transfer to a wire rack to cool completely.

Nutrition Information (per muffin):

✓ Calories: 200

✓ Protein: 12g

✓ Fat: 12g

✓ Carbohydrates: 15g

✓

Conclusion

In conclusion, building and maintaining muscle mass is crucial for overall health and wellness. Incorporating protein-rich ingredients into your diet can help support muscle growth and repair. The recipes in this cookbook provide a delicious way to boost your protein intake and support your muscle-building goals. Whether you're looking for a post-workout snack, a healthy dessert option, or simply a nutritious meal, these recipes are sure to satisfy. So, get in the kitchen, whip up some muscle-boosting treats, and enjoy the benefits of a protein-packed diet!